My
Gymnastics Journal

Keeping Track of The
Ups and Downs!

This Journal Belongs To

_____

Important Note

Do not use permanent markers or Sharpie pens in this book as the ink will bleed through the page. Ballpoint pen or pencil is best.

Published by K. Francklin

Cover Image: Produced by K. Francklin

Image License Purchased © Can Stock Photo Inc. / [KinoMasterskaya]

ISBN-13: 978-1530703388

ISBN-10: 1530703387

All about Me!

My Gymnastics Club: _____

My Coach: _____

Number of hours a week I train: _____

Total number of medals:

	I already have	I want to have
Gold		
Silver		
Bronze		

The badge/grade/level I am training towards:

_____

_____

The apparatus I am best on: _____

Apparatus I like the best: _____

The apparatus I need to work on most: _____

My best friend(s) at gym: _____

_____

Current age: _____

My Ideal Leotard Design

Front

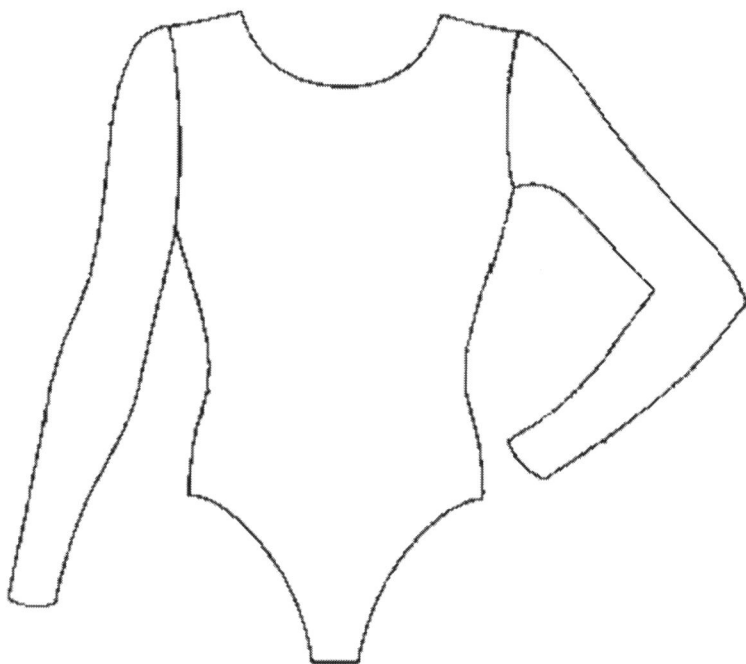

My Ideal Leotard Design

Back

This Week at Gym

Date: _____

New moves?

Vault	Bars	Beam	Floor

Rewards? _____

_____

_____

Bruises? _____

_____

_____

<u>Notes</u>

Doodle Page

This Week at Gym   Date: _____

New moves?

Vault	Bars	Beam	Floor

Rewards? _____

_____

_____

Bruises? _____

_____

_____

<u>Notes</u>

World Artistic Gymnastics Championships

Event Date: _____

Female Gymnasts I'm Supporting

Gymnast Name	Country

Team I'm Supporting: _____

Results
(Write the Country or Gymnast and Score)

Event	Gold	Silver	Bronze
Team			
Individual (All Round)			
Vault			
Bars			
Beam			
Floor			

This Week at Gym Date: _____

New moves?

Vault	Bars	Beam	Floor

Rewards? _____

_____

_____

Bruises? _____

_____

_____

<u>Notes</u>

Doodle Page

This Week at Gym   Date: _____

New moves?

Vault	Bars	Beam	Floor

Rewards? _____
_____
_____

Bruises? _____
_____
_____

Notes

Let's Split!

How well are your splits going?

Type	Getting There	Almost There	Done It
Right Leg Split			
Left Leg Split			
Box Splits			

This Week at Gym   Date: _____

New moves?

Vault	Bars	Beam	Floor

Rewards? _____
_____
_____

Bruises? _____
_____
_____

Notes

Doodle Page

This Week at Gym   Date: _____

New moves?

Vault	Bars	Beam	Floor

Rewards? _____
_____
_____

Bruises? _____
_____
_____

<u>Notes</u>

Fact File – Women's Gymnastics

Female Gymnast	Interesting Facts

(E.g. date of birth, medals, where they train,
famous moves, ever meet them, best apparatus)

This Week at Gym

Date: _____

New moves?

Vault	Bars	Beam	Floor

Rewards? _____
_____
_____

Bruises? _____
_____
_____

<u>Notes</u>

Doodle Page

This Week at Gym

Date: _____

New moves?

Vault	Bars	Beam	Floor

Rewards? _____

_____

_____

Bruises? _____

_____

_____

Notes

Cool Stuff

This page is for writing down cool gymnastics stuff that you would really like to have! Then you can start saving up for it or offer it as ideas for your Christmas & birthday presents! Be realistic though! ☺

This Week at Gym   Date: _____

New moves?

Vault	Bars	Beam	Floor

Rewards? _____
_____
_____

Bruises? _____
_____
_____

<u>Notes</u>

Doodle Page

This Week at Gym　　　Date: _____

New moves?

Vault	Bars	Beam	Floor

Rewards? _____
_____
_____

Bruises? _____
_____
_____

Notes

Floor & Beam Moves

Tick the box that is relevant to you at the moment. If you do not know what a move is yet then try to find out what that move is and what it looks like. It could be your dream move!

The Move	I Know What This One Is	I'm Learning This One	I Can Do This One
Back Handspring			
Front Handspring			
Backward Somersault			
Forward Somersault			
Cartwheel			
Aerial Cartwheel			
Aerial Walkover			
Round Off			
Straight Jump			
Scissors Leap			
Split Leap			
Front Walkover			
Back Walkover			

This Week at Gym

Date: _____

New moves?

Vault	Bars	Beam	Floor

Rewards? _____

_____

_____

Bruises? _____

_____

_____

Notes

Doodle Page

This Week at Gym   Date: _____

New moves?

Vault	Bars	Beam	Floor

Rewards? _____
_____
_____

Bruises? _____
_____
_____

Notes

Best Friends

Friends at gym are the best – they fully understand and support you so it's time to plan a get together! Make sure you ask your parents permission beforehand though.

Who to invite? _____

_____

_____

When & Where? _____

What to do? _____

_____

_____

_____

Things to bring? _____

_____

_____

_____

_____

Special food needed? _____

_____

_____

_____

This Week at Gym   Date: _____

New moves?

Vault	Bars	Beam	Floor

Rewards? _____

_____

_____

Bruises? _____

_____

_____

Notes

Doodle Page

This Week at Gym

Date: _____

New moves?

Vault	Bars	Beam	Floor

Rewards? _____
_____
_____

Bruises? _____
_____
_____

Notes

Fun Challenges

Can you do the following?

Challenge	Yes/No
Stand on one leg and count to 20 with your eyes closed	
Sit cross legged on the floor and try to stand up without using your hands	
Lace your fingers together and step through with both feet	
Put one or two ankles behind your head while sitting	
Close your eyes and try to touch the tips of your fingers together over your head	
Hold one leg out in front of you and squat all the way down and then return to standing without using your hands	
Try to do a push up and clap while in the air	
Do a headstand. How many times can you clap before losing your balance?	
Lie on your back, fold your arms onto your chest, and then stand up with your arms still folded	

This Week at Gym   Date: _____

New moves?

Vault	Bars	Beam	Floor

Rewards? _____

_____

_____

Bruises? _____

_____

_____

Notes

Doodle Page

This Week at Gym   Date: _____

New moves?

Vault	Bars	Beam	Floor

Rewards? _____
_____
_____

Bruises? _____
_____
_____

Notes

Best Gymnast Ever

Who do you think is the best female gymnast? Which gymnast do you like the most?

Use the space below to write down details of the gymnast who really inspires you and the reasons why. Remember them when things get tough – even the world's top gymnasts have bad days.

This Week at Gym   Date: _____

New moves?

Vault	Bars	Beam	Floor

Rewards? _____
_____
_____

Bruises? _____
_____
_____

Notes

Doodle Page

This Week at Gym

Date: _____

New moves?

Vault	Bars	Beam	Floor

Rewards? _____
_____
_____

Bruises? _____
_____
_____

<u>Notes</u>

Maze

Start

Finish

This Week at Gym   Date: _____

New moves?

Vault	Bars	Beam	Floor

Rewards? _____

_____

_____

Bruises? _____

_____

_____

<u>Notes</u>

Doodle Page

This Week at Gym

Date: _____

New moves?

Vault	Bars	Beam	Floor

Rewards? _____

_____

_____

Bruises? _____

_____

_____

<u>Notes</u>

The Word Is...

See how many different words you come up with from the word: **GYMNASTICS**

1.	23.
2.	24.
3.	25.
4.	26.
5.	27.
6.	28.
7.	29.
8.	30.
9.	31.
10.	32.
11.	33.
12.	34.
13.	35.
14.	36.
15.	37.
16.	38.
17.	39.
18.	40.
19.	41.
20.	42.
21.	43.
22.	44.

This Week at Gym   Date: _____

New moves?

Vault	Bars	Beam	Floor

Rewards? _____

_____

_____

Bruises? _____

_____

_____

Notes

Update about Me!

My Gymnastics Club: _____

My Coach: _____

Number of hours a week I train: _____

Total number of medals:

	I now have	But I really want
Gold		
Silver		
Bronze		

The badge/grade/level I am training towards:

_____

_____

The apparatus I am now best on: _____

Apparatus I like the best: _____

The apparatus I now need to work on is: _____

Current date: _____

Current age: _____

This Week at Gym

Date: _____

New moves?

Vault	Bars	Beam	Floor

Rewards? _____
_____
_____

Bruises? _____
_____
_____

Notes

Doodle Page

This Week at Gym   Date: _____

New moves?

Vault	Bars	Beam	Floor

Rewards? _____
_____
_____

Bruises? _____
_____
_____

Notes

Fact File – Men's Gymnastics

Male Gymnast	Interesting Facts

(E.g. date of birth, medals, where they train,
ever meet them, best apparatus)

This Week at Gym

Date: _____

New moves?

Vault	Bars	Beam	Floor

Rewards? _____
_____
_____

Bruises? _____
_____
_____

<u>Notes</u>

Doodle Page

This Week at Gym

Date: _____

New moves?

Vault	Bars	Beam	Floor

Rewards? _____
_____
_____

Bruises? _____
_____
_____

<u>Notes</u>

Hair Styles

Sketch your competition hair style ideas but keep in mind:

- Will it stay secure?
- Will it be distracting?
- Can you do all moves with it? (E.g. backward roll)

This Week at Gym   Date: _____

New moves?

Vault	Bars	Beam	Floor

Rewards? _____
_____
_____

Bruises? _____
_____
_____

<u>Notes</u>

Doodle Page

This Week at Gym   Date: _____

New moves?

Vault	Bars	Beam	Floor

Rewards? _____
_____
_____

Bruises? _____
_____
_____

<u>Notes</u>

Books

When gymnasts retire they often write a book about their achievements. Sometimes they write one before retiring! Check out if the gymnasts you love or support have written something and write the details down.

Book Title	Author	Seller	Price

This Week at Gym   Date: _____

New moves?

Vault	Bars	Beam	Floor

Rewards? _____
_____
_____

Bruises? _____
_____
_____

<u>Notes</u>

Doodle Page

This Week at Gym   Date: _____

New moves?

Vault	Bars	Beam	Floor

Rewards? _____
_____
_____

Bruises? _____
_____
_____

<u>Notes</u>

Healthy Snacks

Having snacks during or after training is great for keeping your energy levels up. However, not all snacks are good! Your coach may have already given you guidelines on what you can and can't bring to gym.

Do you have any other ideas? What do your friends bring that you might like too? Having the same snack every time can become boring so come up with some other ideas to provide a bit of variety.

This Week at Gym   Date: _____

New moves?

Vault	Bars	Beam	Floor

Rewards? _____
_____
_____

Bruises? _____
_____
_____

<u>Notes</u>

Doodle Page

This Week at Gym   Date: _____

New moves?

Vault	Bars	Beam	Floor

Rewards? _____
_____
_____

Bruises? _____
_____
_____

Notes

Inspirational Quotes

Write down some quotes that really motivate you to keep going and aim high. Can you come up with your own quote?

Quote	Who Said It?

This Week at Gym   Date: _____

New moves?

Vault	Bars	Beam	Floor

Rewards? _____
_____
_____

Bruises? _____
_____
_____

<u>Notes</u>

Doodle Page

This Week at Gym   Date: _____

New moves?

Vault	Bars	Beam	Floor

Rewards? _____
_____
_____

Bruises? _____
_____
_____

Notes

Let's Split Again!

How well are your splits going? Any improvements?

Type	Getting There	Almost There	Done It
Right Leg Split			
Left Leg Split			
Box Splits			

This Week at Gym

Date: _____

New moves?

Vault	Bars	Beam	Floor

Rewards? _____
_____
_____

Bruises? _____
_____
_____

Notes

Doodle Page

This Week at Gym

Date: _____

New moves?

Vault	Bars	Beam	Floor

Rewards? _____
_____
_____

Bruises? _____
_____
_____

<u>Notes</u>

Still Best Friends

Friends at gym are still the best so it's time to plan another get together! Make sure you ask your parents permission beforehand.

Who to invite? _____
_____
_____

When & Where? _____

What to do? _____
_____
_____
_____

Things to bring? _____
_____
_____
_____
_____

Special food needed? _____
_____
_____
_____

This Week at Gym   Date: _____

New moves?

Vault	Bars	Beam	Floor

Rewards? _____
_____
_____

Bruises? _____
_____
_____

Notes

Doodle Page

This Week at Gym   Date: _____

New moves?

Vault	Bars	Beam	Floor

Rewards? _____
_____
_____

Bruises? _____
_____
_____

Notes

Floor Music

Floor music can enhance or detract from your performance so choose carefully. What music reflects your own unique style?

Ideas:

Music I Like	Composer/Writer	Is It Suitable?

This Week at Gym   Date: _____

New moves?

Vault	Bars	Beam	Floor

Rewards? _____
_____
_____

Bruises? _____
_____
_____

<u>Notes</u>

Doodle Page

This Week at Gym   Date: _____

New moves?

Vault	Bars	Beam	Floor

Rewards? _____
_____
_____

Bruises? _____
_____
_____

<u>Notes</u>

Raise the Flag

Draw the country flag of the 2 gymnastics teams you support.

This Week at Gym   Date: _____

New moves?

Vault	Bars	Beam	Floor

Rewards? _____
_____
_____

Bruises? _____
_____
_____

<u>Notes</u>

Doodle Page

This Week at Gym

Date: _____

New moves?

Vault	Bars	Beam	Floor

Rewards? _____
_____
_____

Bruises? _____
_____
_____

<u>Notes</u>

Handstand Test

How long can you hold your handstand? If you can't do handstands yet then how long can you hold a headstand or handstand against a wall?

Time to find out! Ask someone to count how many seconds you can hold your handstand/headstand. Have 5 tries and then use your average result in the table below.

Date of Test	Handstand/Headstand	Time Held

This Week at Gym

Date: _____

New moves?

Vault	Bars	Beam	Floor

Rewards? _____
_____
_____

Bruises? _____
_____
_____

Notes

Doodle Page

This Week at Gym   Date: _____

New moves?

Vault	Bars	Beam	Floor

Rewards? _____
_____
_____

Bruises? _____
_____
_____

<u>Notes</u>

Wordsearch

Find the following words:

Aerial   Pike
Cartwheel   Routine
Flexible   Strength
Giant   Tumbling
Leotard   Vault

H	D	M	B	C	P	E	J	L	V
T	U	R	H	L	A	I	R	E	A
G	F	Q	A	P	R	G	K	H	U
N	C	A	R	T	W	H	E	E	L
E	N	I	T	U	O	R	O	K	T
R	T	W	G	Y	A	E	P	I	C
T	E	L	B	I	X	E	L	F	P
S	V	D	E	G	A	J	W	I	O
T	U	M	B	L	I	N	G	A	X
Z	R	G	P	A	R	C	T	E	T

This Week at Gym   Date: _____

New moves?

Vault	Bars	Beam	Floor

Rewards? _____
_____
_____

Bruises? _____
_____
_____

<u>Notes</u>

Doodle Page

This Week at Gym   Date: _____

New moves?

Vault	Bars	Beam	Floor

Rewards? _____
_____
_____

Bruises? _____
_____
_____

Notes

Inspirational Poster

What You Need:

- Paper
- Fancy card (optional)
- Glue
- Scissors
- Sharpie
- Sticky stuff to put poster on wall
- Access to internet & printer

What to Do:

- Find some photos of gymnasts on the internet and print them out.
- Cut the photos to the desired shape and size.
- Glue the photos onto a large piece of paper to create a poster.
- Use a Sharpie to write some quotes either directly onto the poster or onto fancy card to stick onto the poster.
- Stick onto your wall and be inspired!

This Week at Gym   Date: _____

New moves?

Vault	Bars	Beam	Floor

Rewards? _____
_____
_____

Bruises? _____
_____
_____

<u>Notes</u>

Doodle Page

This Week at Gym

Date: _____

New moves?

Vault	Bars	Beam	Floor

Rewards? _____
_____
_____

Bruises? _____
_____
_____

<u>Notes</u>

Dream Big

Gymnast I would most like to meet (can be past or present):

_____

Leotard I would most like to have (and the price is?):

_____

Vault move I would love to be able to do:

_____

Bar move I would love to be able to do:

_____

Beam move I would love to be able to do:

_____

Floor move I would love to be able to do:

_____

Medal I would most like to win (think BIG!):

_____

This Week at Gym   Date: _____

New moves?

Vault	Bars	Beam	Floor

Rewards? _____
_____
_____

Bruises? _____
_____
_____

Notes

Time to get a new journal and update my awesome progress…

Disclaimer

The use of this journal/diary is intended for gymnasts who are being coached by a professional and so understand and follow safe practice. The author does not accept responsibility for any injuries, losses or damage arising from using this journal.

All Rights Reserved

38812689R00057

Printed in Great Britain
by Amazon